WE DON'T SAY GOODBYE AND NEITHER DO THEY

Instead we say, "see you later!"

CHERYL KAY

We Don't Say Goodbye and Neither Do They: Instead we say, "See you later!"
© Cheryl Kay 2022

ISBN: 978-1-922578-68-6 (paperback)

All rights reserved. No part of this publication may be reproduced, stored in a retrieval system, or transmitted in any form or by any means electronic, mechanical, photocopying, recording, or otherwise, without the prior written permission of the author.

Published in Australia by Cheryl Kay and InHouse Publishing.
www.inhousepublishing.com.au

Printed in Australia by InHouse Print & Design.

A catalogue record for this book is available from the National Library of Australia

I started as a student, now I am an Author, taking dictation from the Spirit world.

— Cheryl Kay

"Our comfortable Spiritual home provides remarkable experiences for us. Using our delightful ethereal Spirit soul energy, we visit your Earth atmosphere regularly, bringing gifts of love and healing."

– Team Spirit

CONTENTS

Dedication vii
Acknowledgements ix
Introduction. xiii

Beginnings 1
Justin and My "Dearest Friend" xoxo. 9
Communicating with the Spirit Realm 17
Transitioning Home to Spirit World. 25
Mediumship 37
Spirit Soul Connections. 45
Spirits Speaking To Me 51
Spirit Speaks. 73
Life/Afterlife 79
Spirit General Meeting. 83

Afterword. 89
To Be Continued 91
Cheryl Kay – Spiritology 95
Master of Ceremonies, Candles, White Sage
and Illumination. 99
Stepping Through the Celestial Doorway. 105
Healing Crystals for Fragile Hearts. 111
Music for Both Sides of the Veil. 115
The Lighthouse Keeper for Unsettled Souls 119
Exploring Helpful Resources. 121

You do not need to edit your writing when Spirit wakes you just before dawn and whispers, "It's time to take down some dictation."

– Cheryl Kay

DEDICATION

Dedicated to the Spirit World – *Life/Afterlife*

When we are ready to move beyond our deep feelings of grief, we open our communication portal with the Spirit world. "We don't say goodbye and neither do they." Instead, we say. "See you later"

– Cheryl Kay

ACKNOWLEDGEMENTS

To everyone who believed and trusted my work, a big group hug! Thank you.

A special thank you to the Spirit Souls who shared their stories with me. xoxo

Congratulations to my Soul for succeeding to stay focused and confident when others tried to shoot me down.

To Justin and my "dearest friend," and my abundance of trusted Spirit World advisors, Spirit guides and Spirited team. Thank you!

I love you all more than words can express. xoxo

A special thank you to everyone in my Spirit Realm family. You have been the guiding light I needed during my times of great sadness and darkness. I am grateful, I am thankful. Love, more love. xoxo

To Justin and my "dearest friend," there will always be a continuous supply of hugs for you both.

I enthusiastically acknowledge the fantastic work accomplishments of my Spirited team and Spirit guides. Their commitment to strengthening the Earth Souls skills to connect and communicate with family and friends in the Spirit Realm has been tremendous.

Our book, memoir, co-created, written with Justin and my "dearest friend." xoxo

Out of respect to people who requested their loved one's identity remain anonymous I have either changed the name or in the case of my "dearest friend" who also co-authored this book, I have referred to her as my "dearest friend" to respect and protect the wishes of her family for privacy.

I could not find a book to help me, so I wrote a book to help me.

– Cheryl Kay

INTRODUCTION

Hello! Greetings, fellow Earth Souls. My name is Cheryl Kay. I've called the Central Coast home for the past 8 years and before that I lived in Central West NSW for over 20 years. Born in Melbourne, raised in Wodonga, my childhood was challenging. Numerous times over the past 60-plus years, I've reminisced with the beautiful Spirits who became my friends and confidantes. As a child I experienced regular visits from people who had no physical bodies. These memories have vividly stayed with me over the past 60-plus years of my life. I didn't realise at the time that it was the beginning of my life as a Spiritual Medium, more commonly referred to as **"Someone who talks to dead people."**

For the past two years, I've been doing my best to complete an unusual project – co-authoring a book with the Spirit World. I have a great desire to create an environment where we can express ourselves openly with the Spirit World without fear of being criticised or stereotyped by society as kooky! We share our physical world with a great many visitors from the Spirit World who endeavour to connect and communicate with us regularly – validation from them that there is **Life/Afterlife**.

I am a believer in **Life/Afterlife**, and this is my truth.

The Spirit World and I have written this book together using easy, uncomplicated language. The chapters are easy to read, an excellent tool for Earth Souls who are looking to establish their link to the Spirit World to communicate and validate messages to and from their family and friends in Spirit. This book offers an opportunity for Earth Souls to recalibrate their communication skills with family and friends who have transitioned back to their Spirit Soul home. I also love to offer knowledge intuitive in nature that may assist your Earth Soul emotionally and spiritually.

We are living in challenging times. Sadly, many Earth Souls have become addicted to an ego-driven lifestyle, which makes them neglect an essential part of their physical Soul's health and growth. Sometimes when I sit and analyse my ability to communicate with the Spirit World, I am overcome with such powerful emotion. It is the truth of my eternal Soul that I wish to share with you.

Spirit speaks

> "Your physical life experience this time around contains a blueprint of living consciously between worlds. The wisdom you inherited for this physical life experience is a precious gift we would like you to share with your fellow Earth Souls."

We don't say goodbye and neither do they. Instead, we say, "See you later!"

xoxo

Introduction

I wrote this book by hand, with handwriting that became an essential part of my blueprint, and which came to me through automatic writing. You may wish to do the same. Consider the following:

* Eliminate noise and distraction.
* Listen and feel the connection.
* Connect with your Spirit Messenger.
* Marvel at the moment you receive personal guidance.

The Spirit World will leave a lasting impression and expression on your Earth Soul.

Your purpose also is to educate and encourage.

As you turn the pages of our beautiful book, Spirit recommends that you frequently pause to allow your Earth Soul to connect with your loved ones in Spirit. Feel your way through the chapters as insightful information flows to you.

I intend to offer information of an intuitive nature that may assist your Earth Soul emotionally and spiritually. My Spiritual Mediumship role also includes taking dictation from the Spirit Realm (channelled automatic writing).

Cheerfully, Cheryl Kay

Seeking a new soul experience, my guardian Angel gently placed me back into the physical realm so I could experience life as a Spiritual gypsy.

– Cheryl Kay

BEGINNINGS

I was born in Melbourne, but my birth mother's plans didn't include me. She placed me in an orphanage – St Joseph's babies' home.

According to the orphanage records, at nine months of age, I was adopted out to a family who lived in regional Victoria.

I remember, from school age there was a change in the family atmosphere. My adoptive mother took a liking to alcohol; beer in particular. She was a lovely caring woman until she became intoxicated. Then she turned into an aggressive, spiteful, cruel drunk. She inflicted physical, emotional and mental abuse on me without any remorse.

There are scars on my body from being kicked and emotional trauma when she would refer to me as her "gutter child." By the age of 16, I was a mental mess from years of abuse, so I packed an overnight bag and walked away from that life.

Into the jungle of life I went. With low self-esteem, no money and limited education, I was unprepared for the future. At the same time, I was also relieved that I had finally left behind the cruelty of the past.

The next chapter in my life was to meet and marry a man 13 years my senior. In hindsight, I have questioned myself as to

my real intention that led to this union. A much-needed father figure perhaps, or just the opportunity to create the family fairy tale that I longed for but never had. The catalyst for the breakdown in our marriage was his thirst for alcohol. He wasn't an aggressive drunk; instead, he often became incoherent and unreliable. Our age difference also presented challenges, as did his love for poker machines.

Nine months after our daughter was born, I packed two bags, one for my daughter and one for myself. We left to start a new life.

Out of the frying pan and into the fire, I started a relationship with a disc jockey I encountered through my line of work. Our relationship developed rapidly. I believed we were rock solid until I received a shattering phone call from a concerned friend hinting that all was not as I perceived. I was heavily pregnant, due to give birth any day. I remember driving myself to the venue where he was working. When I walked in, I could see him passionately kissing a woman, and I felt my heart shatter into a million pieces. They did not notice me until I tapped them both on the shoulder. In shock, the girl ran from the room whilst he uttered the usual male retort, "It's not what you think." Caught red-handed and knowing full well that he was guilty, his denial became amplified.

The relationship was over, as far as I was concerned. I was an emotional mess. I was let down, unsupported during pregnancy and feeling somewhat rejected yet again. For the sake of our precious baby boy, I decided to give the relationship a second try. I rose to this challenge, and we went on to have our

second son. Our relationship appeared steady, although I had my reservations. Two failed relationships were too much to think of at this time.

One morning my world came crashing down. I went in to wake up the boys. My eldest son did not respond to my early morning ritual of tickling. I pulled back the covers to pick him up. His little body was lifeless. I remember screaming, "NO! NO! NO!" There will never be a way for me to describe in words my feelings at that moment. As I write this, I am reliving the shock, fear and anguish I felt. My gorgeous baby boy, Justin, had passed in his sleep.

After the funeral, his father distanced himself from me. He had needs that I could not fill. I was a grieving mother with no family to turn to and no emotional support. I felt broken. His constant berating, telling me to move on, or that "You need a shrink," only damaged myself and our relationship more.

Huge cracks began forming in our relationship: lies followed by lies to cover his original lie, thus building a large web. It wasn't long before I discovered that his excuses for always being late had a familiar theme. Still grieving for our son, nothing he said or did hurt anymore. The defining moment to end the relationship came one morning when I woke up and said, "Pack all your belongings and leave."

His narcissistic parting words would leave me feeling diminished: "You were never that great anyway."

The next few years it was all about my children and myself and the obstacles we would encounter and conquer.

One day in 1988, I met a lovely lady named June. As we conversed with each other, she shared her unique and intriguing experiences as a Psychic Medium. Her calming nature reassured me that she was genuine, as well as being a lovely caring woman. She listened intently to my stories as well, especially my childhood experiences. I told her about my regular visits from people who had no physical bodies, also explaining about my conversations with my son from the other side. These stories validated my already strong belief in **Life/Afterlife** and the Spirit World. Our friendship lasted for many years. Geographically we became distanced from each other, the phone being our only regular connection.

The last time I dropped in on June unannounced, I got the feeling she was withholding something of great concern. She looked weary, but despite my many probing inquiries as to her wellbeing she assured me that she was fine. She was somewhat aloof when she mentioned the pressing need to visit her sister who lived interstate. A $50 note tucked under her pillow was all I could do for her with the announcement of her sudden abrupt travel arrangement. I was openly concerned when she did not answer or return my calls. My decision to drive the long distance to her home would leave me saddened. Her neighbour informed me that she had vacated her unit to spend the last few months of her life with her sister, and that she didn't want me to worry about her. It was heart breaking and disappointing that she had not confided in me about her illness.

June was the most caring woman who would have given her last dollar to those who needed it more. I often reminisce

about the time she arrived at my house unexpectedly with bread and milk. She had painstakingly taken two trains and two buses to reach this destination. She explained emphatically, with a big smile: "I just got the feeling you might need a hand up, my friend."

June is the same in Spirit, randomly offering me helpful solutions and guidance. Thank you, June, my friend!

Not realising it at the time, June was my Earth Soul teacher. June was my mentor, assisting me in understanding my future role. It was then that I began my life as a Spiritual Medium.

During my childhood, the family I lived with often referred to me as their child with a wild imagination. They reprimanded me often for telling outrageous tales. There were many nights when the Spirit Realm visited me. There were crowds of them, gathering next to my face as I dozed off to sleep. They would chatter to me – sometimes all at once. I thought they were clever, and I often wondered who they were. This, I have come to realise, is because Spirits visit when your body is relaxed, in meditation or asleep. They see this as the perfect time to communicate.

Growing up, I established great respect for their messages and for how they communicated with me. As a child, I would lie in my bed, talking to the Spirits. I welcomed their friendship, their thoughtfulness, their kindness. I liked that they didn't consider me strange; they affirmed my uniqueness.

I still have lovely memories of the way they communicated with me. I could see them and hear them in my head. I did not understand them. They appeared to be talking amongst

themselves but with reference to me. Sometimes they touched my face, hair and arms. Their energy was kind and friendly, therefore I was not afraid. They loved being descriptive and colourful; beautiful shades of yellow, orange, blue, green, red, indigo and violet.

As a kid, they fascinated me with their energy. Countless times, I'd incur the wrath of others who complained of my impulsive, restless behaviour. I tried to explain that it was my Spirit friends who gave me some of their colourful energy. Spending time with them was always loads of fun.

These days, I'm not so frank and open about my energy sources/resources that come to me, compliments of my Spirit guides.

My family often tell me how exhausted they feel being around me, randomly remarking how hard it is to keep up with me. This is because I pick up on the Spirit World's energy; they help me to recharge my energy aura. With a smile and laughter that echoes from deep within my Earth Soul, I often say to them, **"I have friends in high places!"**

Numerous times over the past 60-plus years, I've reminisced with many Spirit Souls who have become my friends and confidantes.

My "dearest friend" worked for me for several years. I always thought of her as a special Earth Angel. She had this angelic, graceful, caring way about her. I would often say, **"Everyone loves you; you're a special soul."** The tragedy of her death in 2015 at the young age of 26 was excruciatingly painful.

The cruelty that the perpetrator inflicted on her was horrific. I kept thinking of her family. There were just no words, and my only way to express my love to her departed Soul was through tears. She regularly visits me and tells me, "***We're still friends. I'm here to help your Earth Soul.***"

She explains further by saying, "You're a wonderful Spiritual Medium. You're great at helping people connect with loved ones in Spirit. I have many messages to share with my family and friends, so can you please pass them on, on my behalf?" xoxo

I've successfully established a healthy communication and validation link with the Spirit Realm. At 60-plus years of age, some people now consider me mysterious, rather than weird! I live happily and comfortably between the two realms of the Earth and Spirit World with ***love and more love. xoxo***

My heart experienced the true depth of my love for you when I confronted the anguish of your Earth soul's departure.

– Cheryl Kay

In the Spirit world's book of life, an Angel wrote a heartfelt message next to my son's birthdate. "Precious little soul, your stay in the Earth's atmosphere will be brief, the love you'll share with your mum will be forever, eternal."

– Cheryl Kay

JUSTIN AND MY "DEAREST FRIEND" xoxo

J oie de vivre describes the exultation (rejoicing) of the Spirit World.

Justin, my adorable son, and my "dearest friend" both transitioned back to their Spiritual home at young ages. Justin was 2; my "dearest friend" was 26. I love both so much; there are no words to describe the bonds we share. We've written this book together while living between two worlds, the Spirit Realm and the Earth's atmosphere.

The three of us have encountered many situations where we have been able to assist with healing on both sides of life: Earth Souls and Spirit Souls.

These rendezvous signalled the beginnings of the first draft of our book back in 2019.

We aim to create an innovative piece of writing – a helpful, easy-to-read guide for Earth Souls.

> **We don't say goodbye and neither do they.**
> **Instead, we say, "See you later!"**
>
> *xoxo*

Justin

I communicate with Spirit Souls.

    What and who is a Spirit Soul? When we experience physical life, we are Earth Souls existing in a physical Earth atmosphere.

When we transition back to our Spiritual home, we transform back into the form of Spirit Soul: delightful, colourful energy residing in the Spirit World.

Communicating with the Spirit World comes easily to me. I sense, see and feel their presence, and I am happy to translate and share knowledge – messages from the Spirit Realm.

Assisting the Spirit World is healing and rewarding for others, including me.

I share messages, stories and communications with loved ones remaining in the Earth's atmosphere.

The Spirit World often comes to me with insightful communication that can be beautiful to witness. They have passed on many messages to me through their unique communication style.

*

The Spirit World's insightful communication:

Death is an Earth Soul's transformation back to their Spiritual home.

Depart Earth's Atmosphere Transition Home:
D = Depart
E = Earth's
A = Atmosphere
T = Transition
H = Home

My personal knowledge of Life/Afterlife – DEATH: Depart Earth's Atmosphere Transition Home.

During my current life here in the Earth's atmosphere, I've experienced the transitions of several family and friends. Two of these transitions had an enormous emotional impact on my Earth Soul. They were the transitions of my son Justin, aged 2 years, 3 months and 22 days, and also my "dearest friend." She was a young Earth Soul aged 26.

On both occasions, for weeks, months and years, there were no words to express the sadness I felt. There was a continuous pain in my heart that felt never-ending. There were never enough tissues on hand to wipe away my tears. Still now, there are times when I openly cry. Grieving is a way of coping and expressing that we still love and miss their physical presence.

Watching me from his Spirit home, Justin tried to connect with me. However, because of my grief, I was not aware of his communication or the love that flowed to me from his precious Spirit Soul heart. Patiently, Justin waited until my deep pain subsided.

One day I woke up and decided to seek the help of a well-respected Psychic Medium in Orange, Central West NSW. I was hopeful that she could make a connection and share with me a message from my son.

Sara had decades of experience and was extraordinarily successful in connecting people with their loved ones who had departed from the physical world. As soon as I settled into the comfortable chair provided, without any hesitation Sara began describing Justin to me. She asked me if I understood why I

regularly stroked the side of my face in a particular pattern. I explained to Sara that I always felt like there was something there. I touched my face in recognition of the feeling. Sara explained to me that Justin was showing her how he gently strokes the side of my face. This is something Justin did as a toddler; he would sit on my lap, stroke my face and give me big hugs. In his sweet voice he would whisper to me, "**It will be okay, Mummy. I love you.**" Justin was such an intuitive child. He loved being affectionate, giving beautiful hugs. Kisses on my forehead were his speciality. After planting a kiss, he would giggle with such delight. I loved those precious moments back then, and now I love and treasure them even more. Love flowed continually from his little Earth Soul. He had an incredible sixth sense for his age. My relationship with his father at the time was at an all-time low and I believe Justin felt my sadness.

Sara's visual description and demonstration were correct. She showed me accurate validation of his presence. A beautiful deep emotion rose from within me; I felt the closeness of his Spirit Soul next to me.

When we completed the consultation, I thanked Sara. She poignantly replied to me, "**Your little boy loves you and he will continue to be part of your life; it's just different now.**" I understood her and, for a moment, I wished for his physical presence so that I could hug him. Immediately, I felt his gentle touch as he stroked the side of my face.

Since that day with Sara, Justin and I have spent the years together, only separated by the thin veil that exists between the

Earth and Spirit World. Justin is always a heartbeat, a thoughtful moment and a gentle touch away. The warmth in his smile is still a welcoming highlight of my day. His carefree smile oozes so much love.

Justin loved to display his absolute joy of me being his Mum. My two-year-old son gave me a beautiful gift. It was the gift of eternal love, giving and receiving love unconditionally.

People use the word unconditional without fully understanding or appreciating the real meaning of the term. My heart feels the real sense of this phrase every day that I get to experience Justin's love unconditionally, with no strings attached.

My "dearest friend" connected with me the night of her brutal death. Initially, I thought I had been dreaming of her. She looked beautiful; she was sitting on an ornate chair dressed in a stunning pink dress. The next day when I heard the news she was missing, I realised she had visited me as a Spirit Soul.

Dialling her mobile number, I begged, **"Please answer. Please don't let this be what I'm sensing, seeing and feeling."**

Everyone was holding on to the hope of her being found alive. I felt a distinct screaming in my head at the realisation that she had transitioned. My "dearest friend" was no longer here in the Earth's atmosphere.

In the following days and weeks, her Spirit Soul kept visiting me, sharing details of what had happened to her, urging me to document the information she told me and showed me for a later timeframe that might assist investigators working on her murder case.

Those days and weeks were some of the most challenging days of my life. It was so heart breaking to know what had happened to her.

My "dearest friend" and I have agreed there is no need to go into any of the details of how she transitioned. Instead, we will focus on the gift of our continuing friendship.

It took considerable time for me to work through my grief. Being so emotionally involved, it tore my heart to pieces. I continued to process all the details she was conveying to me. All the while, my "dearest friend" kept communicating, assuring me she was safe now and I would learn from her.

My "dearest friend" lovingly describes herself as an ethereal energy Spirit teacher in the Spirit World, teaching, mentoring and providing guidance to both realms – the Spirit World and the Earth's atmosphere.

We don't say goodbye and neither do they. Instead, we say, "See you later!"

xoxo

Create space, open your mind, and collaborate with the Spirit world.

– Cheryl Kay

COMMUNICATING WITH THE SPIRIT REALM

Justin and my "dearest friend" have shown great patience while teaching me how to communicate with them using inspirational methods of communication that I admire tremendously. I genuinely feel their expressions of love for me every day. They touch my heart and make their presence felt, showing me gestures of love through their ethereal Spirit bodies.

This new communication style we've established flows lovingly, patiently and sometimes with a little humour, which is typical of their personalities. They inspire me every day to look for, and to look forward to their messages. Our communication signals have developed and matured over the years. The information I now receive is the indisputable proof of their continuing existence after their transitions: **Life/Afterlife.**

I connect and communicate with both daily. I love and cherish the visits.

We don't say goodbye and neither do they. Instead, we say, "See you later!"

xoxo

Connecting to the energy of the Spirit world through Clairvoyance, Clairsentience, Clairaudience, Claircognizance, Clairalience and Clairgustance.

Justin and my "dearest friend" advise me there are an abundant number of Spirit Souls who try every day to connect with their loved ones in the Earth's atmosphere. Their experiences reveal that there are a lot of difficulties in forming a communication link with the Earth's atmosphere.

The Spirit World has enquired as to how we can get our loved ones, family and friends in the Earth's atmosphere to listen and communicate with us. Their urgent plea reminds me of just how fortunate I am to have such a great relationship with their world.

Without hesitation, I offer my help. We can work together as a team, educating and connecting Earth Souls and Spirit Souls.

This book, along with my Spiritual Mediumship, is my way of offering service to the Spirit World Souls.

The Spirit World is excited by my offer and instantly begins to send through messages; information starts to flow. We agree our first project will be this book, our little book of communications written by Spirit Justin, Spirit "dearest friend," myself and a lot of Spirits and Angels who gather regularly in my lounge room offering their inspirational thoughts of **Life/Afterlife**.

Throughout the book, we will share with you some of our experiences. Also, we will provide you with some helpful tips on how Spirit Souls and Earth Souls can connect and stay connected with each other.

*

Without any need for an introduction a Spirit steps forward in a flurry of energy.

"I have a message to share. It will be helpful if you Earth Souls could understand the varying ways a Soul may transition and the impact it has on those family and friends left behind."

Brilliant, I'll make a cuppa and open a new packet of Justin's favourite biscuits, Jam tartlets. I'm ready for a rendezvous – an evening of chatter with the Spirit World in my lounge room.

There are Spirits and Angels in my lounge room.

Another Spirit slowly edges forward in my crowded lounge room. Excited, he begins:

"My time, my life experiences were complete; it was time for me to return to my Spiritual home. An important task I had to complete on my arrival home was to review my growth and development from life as a physical Earth Soul. I love to send my family and friends healing ethereal love in the form of colourful energy. It feels like a burst of sunshine on their skin. Whenever they feel this incredible warmth, I want them to remember just how much I love them."

Perfect; what a lovely way for this Spirit Soul to reach out to his family and friends. After a little probing, I learn that this Spirit Soul has only recently transitioned. A gentle Soul. He tells me his name is Jerry.

The next Soul to step forward is a little more forthright in his mannerisms – a male Spirit who appears to have rehearsed his speech. Without hesitation, he shows me his written speech as he marches to the podium, confident in giving his narrative sermon.

"To communicate with us in the Spirit World, you need an open mind; you must be receptive to our thinking. We exist in another dimension, in another form. Adapt to our thinking in our unique communication style."

He then proceeds to show me an invoice. He keeps referring to the invoice as a bill. Okay, are you trying to tell me your name is Bill? YES! Bill then goes on to share his instructions on how he believes we Earth Souls can connect to the Spirit World easily using his method.

There are high fives all around my jam-packed lounge room of Spirit Souls. They all loved Bill's input and my interpretation of his communication. What follows is my understanding of Bill's instructions.

Bill's methodology

"Find yourself a quiet place, sit comfortably and concentrate.

To open your connection to the Spirit World, send your thoughts, your message, out into the universe. You can do this in several ways.

1) *Quietly and silently (to still one's mind, close the chatter in your head).*
2) *Revisit a memory (think of a positive memory relating to the subject).*
3) *Crying or singing (an emotional form of connection).* [Justin and I often connect this way.]

There is no right or wrong way. Take a personal approach.

An important note here for everyone; it needs to come from the heart, rather than the ego.

Spirit Souls will respond and communicate with you through a feeling or any of your five senses: sight, touch, smell, taste or hearing.

Allow yourself to connect to their energy."

There are many ways you might feel yourself connecting to the energy of the Spirit World.

Bill goes on to give an example of how he connects with his family and friends.

"You feel a warmth that extends throughout your body. This emotional connection is evidence of the presence of a loved one from the Spirit Realm. Initially, you may not recognise or comprehend their unique communication style. Be patient with the Spirit Soul and yourself while you establish your novel way of communicating without barriers, without boundaries.

If you're thinking of one Spirit Soul and another Spirit Soul comes forward, it means their signal is stronger!"

Sometimes the connection may come as "goosebumps" or "spinning" (the faster the spin, the better the connection). My quickest method of connection is like a spinning top. I quickly recognise that they are reaching out to converse with me.

I love how precise Bill is with his input. He is an experienced, no-nonsense communicator!

A significant reminder for us all – it's important to understand that we should not summon a Spirit Soul, but rather send out loving thoughts seeking a connection to communicate.

The next Spirit Soul to step forward is Georgia; she steps forward quietly as a young Soul, offering her thoughtful interpretation to connecting and communicating. She is a gentle Soul.

"To explain my communication technique, I'm a gentle breeze that you'll feel whenever my Spirit Soul is around. I love to float around caressing and whispering my healing words to Earth Souls. I have lots of family and friends I regularly visit. However, I also like to continue with my humanitarian work, so I can be of assistance to Earth Souls who need a helping Angel's winged hug."

So beautifully put, Georgia; I will recommend that anyone in need of a Spirit Soul hug to reach out to you.

When you hear a whisper in your ear, it's a spirit guide's comforting vocalist. "Lovely lady, I'm here for you every day."

– Cheryl Kay

TRANSITIONING HOME TO SPIRIT WORLD

The Spirit World and I have enjoyed each other's company over the past 22 months of 2019 to April 2021 as we discussed the writing of our book. It's been a privilege working alongside the Spirit World. An opportunity for us to learn from each other presented itself early on during the first draft of this book.

The Spirit World was eager for me to learn about death from their perspective, a transition from one atmosphere to another. The Spirit World longs for the day when we fully comprehend this. It will enable masses of Spirit Souls to communicate freely with family and friends still living in the Earth's atmosphere. The current opportunity for communication is limited because of our closed minds – not believing there is a connection between the two realms.

During one discussion, I took many notes as they enthusiastically explained different departures/transitions to me. A lot of Spirit Souls popped in for a chat, offering their input and personal experiences about their transitions, their departures and crossing over. I was in awe of the intricate details of their experiences. Some Spirit Souls spoke of their horrifying

ordeals relating to their transitions. Each of their stories was complex, leaving a lasting emotional impression on me of just how powerful the evidence they presented to me was – that there is **Life/Afterlife**.

A message from a Spirit:

"The love we shared in the physical world transcends with our Soul to our Spiritual home. The expression that love is eternal, is correct. Without judgement, you, the Earth Soul, need to be more conscious of our ability to connect with you, and also how we connect with you after our transition. Your lack of response and constant emitting of busy signals to our messages wreaks havoc with our Spiritual energy. Mediumship demonstrations take place all over the world connecting Earth and Spirit Souls with the messages, healing and validation that there is Life/Afterlife. It may surprise you to read this. Your family and friends in the Spirit World visit you regularly. They leave hints of their visits, often lovingly wrapping their Soul energy around you. They are gentle in the delivery of their message so as not to freak you out."

Transitioning, or crossing over as some people prefer to say, is an individual experience, a journey to **Life/Afterlife**.

As the Earth Soul begins its transitional journey home, the prana (air) leaves the physical body. Our five senses – sight, smell,

taste, touch and hearing – diminish one by one in the order in which I've written them.

Spending time with a loved one as they prepare for their transition is a Spiritual experience for the Earth Soul. As their Earth Soul transcends back to the Spirit World, they take with them a lasting memory: their last moments with you; your touch, your words.

Your last touch and last words are of comfort to them – a heartfelt keepsake – as they enter the departure area for their journey back to their Spiritual home.

We don't say goodbye and neither do they. Instead, we say, "See you later!"

xoxo

Spirit Souls are eager to share their evidence with you so you can develop a better understanding that there is **Life/Afterlife**. It is also important to reiterate that the messages they send leave no uncertainty; they do start a new life without a physical body.

*

The Spirit World is keen to discuss examples of transitioning. Here are some of their experiences that they would like to share.

Peaceful transition

"My Earth Soul had completed its physical life journey. Along the way, I achieved my personal

goals, evolving as an Earth Soul, living in the Earth's atmosphere. I received a signal at the Earth age of 99: 'It's time for your departure; you have outgrown your Earth Soul's physical body. Mentally and emotionally, you have surpassed your learning goals in this Earth life cycle.'

"My transition back to my Spirit home was memorable. My last moments of life were shared with a lot of my family by my side. One by one I hugged them and whispered my personal goodbye. My transition was peaceful."

The Transition of our Soul back to our Spiritual home"
DEATH – Depart Earth Atmosphere Transition Home.

Sleep-time transition

"My Earth Soul spent time quietly meditating on the pending journey. I spent valuable time sending loving thoughts to my family and friends as it became more evident that my transition was nearing. My attention and focus then shifted to my Spirit Soul family. They had gathered and were patient, as they waited for my Earth Soul to begin the journey home.

The Earth Soul described the walkway to the Spirit Realm as picturesque, describing the process as heavenly, with fairy lights, stars and the pathway lit up with beautiful moonlight."

Daytime transition

"My Earth Soul sensed that my departure time had arrived the moment I woke up that morning. I wasn't afraid or anxious. I had lived a beautiful, elegant life. My lifestyle had graced me with gifts that I had lovingly and openly shared with others less fortunate than myself.

Being an avid follower of the Spirit Realm, I waited patiently for some family and friends to come to visit me and prepare me for the journey.

When I felt them standing with me, they assured me that I wouldn't be making the journey home alone. The reassurance was welcome as was the welcome home party that was awaiting my arrival.

With my goodbyes completed, I gathered my precious memories, then slowly let the prana (air) leave my physical body, homeward bound."

Gradual transition

[The Spirit World's memo to any Earth Soul with a health issue.] *"My Earth Soul body had a disease attached to it. I required both physical and emotional healing before my transition. With regret, I had to admit to my Soul that during my life journey, I had neglected the opportunity to be more fruitful. Unfortunate for me, because I had wasted this Earth Soul life by not evolving as I had envisaged. Instead, I fell back into my old ways of unresolved issues and bitter resentment.*

The Spirit World had frequently visited me; they continually offered support on how to learn and heal in this life. They continued to do this the whole time I was living a physical presence as an Earth Soul in the Earth's atmosphere. Patiently, they continued to hover around my Earth Soul waiting for my signal of readiness to be escorted back to my Spiritual home. The moment I stepped through to the light, all my disease and physical pain disappeared. My incomplete learning still had to be addressed. My life review of my mind, body and Spirit included the

effect the disease had had on my physical body and how I had created barriers for my Soul's growth."

Some Souls are incredibly reluctant to leave the Earth's atmosphere. Many examples of this come from Earth Souls who have transitioned due to horrific circumstances. They try to assist in seeking justice. The need to comfort their distraught family and friends is essential to them. Staying connected is of considerable significance to them. The Spirit World also refers to this gradual transition as an incomplete transition.

Traumatic transition

"The traumatic departure of an Earth Soul is hard for Earth Souls to comprehend. When there has been a murder or fatal accident, the Soul departs the Earth's atmosphere unprepared for the journey home."

These Souls depart the Earth's atmosphere due to events that end their physical lives, with murder being the most common.

It is not uncommon for some of these Souls to be reluctant to leave the Earth's atmosphere. Often, they'll try to reconnect with their loved ones still in the Earth's atmosphere, with a longing to help them through their grieving. They're confused about how to communicate with their family and friends they've left behind.

Many Souls who have experienced traumatic departures will try to assist their families with information relating to their traumatic separation. These Souls seek the help of a Spiritual

Medium who can tune in to their frequency and pass on urgent messages to family and friends.

Incomplete transition

In incomplete transitions, the Earth Soul doesn't complete its transition to the light and the love of the Spirit World. Instead, they stay close to the Earth's atmosphere and their familiar surrounds. They have unfinished business, such as the need to resolve differences; a rift in the family; monetary problems; or conversations they need to complete.

Part of our work as Spirit Mediums is to encourage these Souls to complete their journey. A completed transition means a better connection from the other side, enabling them to resolve any unfinished business.

There are often mitigating circumstances surrounding a Soul who is reluctant to complete their transition. I have encountered some Souls who were in this situation. They've been happy to share their stories, further along in this book.

Early transition

Some Earth Souls struggle to exist in the Earth's atmosphere. These Souls retreat to their Spiritual home into the embrace of Spirit Souls who have already transitioned. They choose an early exit. Many of these Souls have endured enormous pain, both mentally and physically.

Those left behind grieving the loss of these Souls have trouble trying to understand their decisions to leave.

The Spirit World steps forward with some of these Souls who want to share their journeys with us:

"We are back, safe in our Spiritual home; we transitioned early. Please don't judge us. We share some of our stories with you further along in this book."

Our Earth society has varying opinions on those who transition early.

Connecting with these Souls in their Spiritual home, they share stories of their Earth life without malice or revenge. They share from an ethereal energy source experience.

We don't say goodbye and neither do they. Instead, we say, "See you later!"

xoxo

Assisted transition

An Earth Soul, for a variety of reasons, may choose not to pass through to the light to their Spiritual home. Instead, their energy field tries to continue to exist in the Earth's atmosphere. These Souls wholeheartedly believe in their choices. Often, they have unfinished business, (similar to those who have an incomplete transition) but choose to stay anyway.

These Souls exhaust themselves of energy trying to exist in an atmosphere that is no longer theirs, frightened of the unknown or just unsure where to go next.

As a Spirit Medium, I've had the pleasure of meeting quite a few of these Souls. Their stories and validation of existence after

their physical departures are unique, inspiring and sometimes heart-wrenching.

Building a strong relationship to help these Souls is my primary focus. Being patient allows me to explain the necessity and benefits of a full transition home. They can connect and communicate more effectively with family and friends after the transition. Assisting these Souls is extremely rewarding for me. The Spirit Soul experiences greater agility and ability to connect and communicate with loved ones they leave behind when they transition.

The ceremony etiquette of our assisted transitions is described in detail under the headings "Master of Ceremonies, candles, white sage and illumination" and "Stepping through the celestial doorway."

Spirit Souls and Earth Souls also share their experiences and perspectives, respectively.

Archangels

Archangels Azrael and Jeremiel are part of a transition team that assist our Earth Soul during transition and after transition. These two archangels assist both the Earth Soul who is grieving and the Spirit Soul who is or has recently transitioned.

Archangel Azrael

Archangel Azrael opens the door into a new life: an expansion of consciousness; new realms. We also know him as the Angel of comfort as he escorts Souls back to their Spiritual home.

Archangel Azrael assists every Earth Soul in the process of their departure/transition. He can also provide help in unexpected ways to anyone grieving the loss of a loved one.

Azrael's presence in our lives as we grieve the loss of a loved one resembles a lighthouse lantern that gently sweeps across an ocean, guiding ships at sea. In a rhythmic movement in the night's stillness, Azrael becomes our guiding light.

If you are with a loved one in the last stages of transition, it's not uncommon to feel Azrael's non-physical presence. Often people will recall a moment, a feeling, that they didn't understand as they said their goodbyes to a loved one. It always transpires it was Azrael assisting both the Spirit Soul transitioning and the Earth Soul witnessing their loved one's transition.

Archangel Jeremiel

Archangel Jeremiel helps Souls to complete their Earth life reviews. He provides support and guidance during the review process.

Every Soul returning to the Spirit World completes a revision. Archangel Jeremiel assists in highlighting different areas and experiences that the Soul lived as an Earth Soul that require reflection/review.

Common areas for evaluation are relationships, significant achievements, lessons mastered and lessons rejected.

Meditation functions like a latchkey. Beautiful sound exudes when the key opens the door and your Spirit guide welcomes you in – Let's talk.

– Cheryl Kay

MEDIUMSHIP

An evening of Mediumship with Louise Hermann, 14 February 2020

Louise Hermann holds her Mediumship nights monthly at various locations – Sydney, Newcastle and Central Coast. Because of my work commitments, it had been impossible for me to attend regularly. On this occasion, I wouldn't be working. Therefore, I was looking forward to spending an evening amongst Spirit family and friends.

The three of us (Justin, my "dearest friend" and I) made our way to the venue. As I drove, they fogged up my windows with their excited energy; it was hilarious. I was looking forward to an evening with the Spirits.

Louise's Mediumship events involve an evening of connecting with Spirit messages and conversations, healing meditations and inspirational speech. The first of her Spirit visitors on this night came through to send love and healing to me.

A transcript written exactly how the Spirit communicated with Louise:

"I have here with me a female, male and Scott.

The male is like a brother figure to the female. The male, passed some time back, [March] is like a brother to the female. [repeats this to emphasise]

Justin transitioned in March.

Scott makes things with his hands.

The three lived life to the full.

Lung failure – head, neck, lungs – these areas contributed to their deaths, separately, collectively."

This was validation for me – these were all contributing factors in each of their transitions; Justin, my "dearest friend" and Scott.

"Scott expresses 'I lived life to the full'."

Validation – This was a cryptic message for Scott's wife, which only she could validate, and she did.

Male in Spirit: *"I have a brother still living; I hang out with him regularly."*

Validation – Justin with his brother Lou.

"The male wants to give me a big hug."

Validation – Justin.

"Big birthday dates around the departure of the males."

Validation – Justin passed on his father's birthday and his sister's birthday was the day after. Scott died four days before his wife's birthday.

"An understanding that I have a high level of Spiritual faith."

Validation – This is 100 per cent true.

"A male spending time with me every day."

Validation – Yes, that is true; the male spirit companion being my son, Justin. This is evidence that Justin and I have a great relationship between realms.

There is a female Spirit present: *"She is expressing her inability to show her love when she was alive. Since her passing, she has connected with a male Spirit related to you, also passed over. She tells me she is trying to make amends for how she treated you when she was alive by caring for this male Spirit Soul associated with you. She wants you to know it's important to her."*

Validation – This female Spirit is my adopted mother; I understand the message Louise is giving me. It is also interesting to note that when my adopted mother transitioned and completed her life review, she was able to express remorse for the way she treated me.

"A quilt, how to make one. It is American."

Validation – Unable to validate as I have no idea of the context of this message. Sometimes a Spirit gives a future glimpse of what is to be.

"Odd remark." – says Louise – *"Vegetarian?"*

Validation – It obviously has been noted by the Spirit World that I have changed my diet. I eat less meat these days.

"Your gut has been out of balance for the past two years. You have been working on yourself to rebalance on all levels."

Validation – Definite validation.

"The last couple of years, you've been out of balance."

Validation – This is true as I am continually trying to pull together a more peaceful life. I understand the message Louise is giving me.

"Go two doors down. A place of interest. Two doors down."

Louise walks sideways to show two doors down.

"They've met up."

Validation – It's a personal cryptic message.

"I'm safe; please believe this."

Validation – A message from my "dearest friend."

"A lot of laughter."

"I've ended up where I should be."

"Leprechaun or unicorn?"

Validation – Louise mentioned that there would be a symbol trying to get my attention. It will be significant in some way.

"There is a male and female Spirit standing behind you, helping each other to put a necklace around your neck."

Validation – Justin and my "dearest friend."

"These same male and female Spirits love to cling to your back like monkeys, giving you big hugs."

Validation – I could relate to this message. Justin loved to climb up on my back like a monkey and I remember my "dearest friend" loved to creep up from behind and hug me.

"For you, there will be more dreams, more fun and joy arriving in your life."

"A valentine rose, short-stemmed, sent with a lot of love."

Validation – Justin offering me a short-stemmed white rose. I often place a beautifully perfumed white rose near his photo as a gift to him from me.

We don't say goodbye and neither do they. Instead, we say, "See you later!"

xoxo

Validation of the Spirit visitors

Listening to Louise speak with the Spirit World, I realised who the three Spirit Souls were that had been communicating with her.

They were my son Justin, my "dearest friend" and Scott.

I put my hand up as acknowledgement to Louise that she had found a recipient for Scott, the name she put out to the audience as the Spirit visitor with her. I acknowledge to Louise that I know Scott. I don't mention the names of the other two Spirit Souls Louise is describing. Louise prefers for Spirits to validate who they are. Her platform as a Medium is genuine authenticity.

I listen and receive the healing messages from Justin, my "dearest friend" and Scott.

It's important to discuss the reason that Scott was the initial spokesperson to come through.

Scott and I had discussed **Life/Afterlife** before he transitioned. I recollect our conversation. I remember seeing and feeling the full extent of his sadness – his grief – at losing his beautiful daughter. She had transitioned at the young age of 26 through horrific circumstances. Scott could not relate to my theory, as he politely put it. Communicating with the dead seemed far-fetched to him.

After her transition, my "dearest friend" spent a lot of time around her father, trying to connect, trying to help him. He was struggling to comprehend his grief.

We don't say Goodbye and neither do they" Instead we say. "See you later!"

Scott has now transitioned through to the light. He is very demonstrative of the fact that he now understands how easy it is to communicate with his family and friends still living in the Earth's atmosphere. Scott wanted to let me know that he now understands the conversations and messages we had, back when he was a physical Earth Soul.

The special meaning and validation of these messages from Louise are beautiful. I have had many visits from my son. Justin loves to tell me how proud of me he is, and of how he loves to hug me, just like I used to hug him when he was a little boy. He's still cuddly with his loving energy, exactly like he was in his physical life form.

It is always a profound experience when someone else connects to Justin's Spirit Soul, delivering me messages of love and healing.

The bond is stronger since they've gone home to the Spirit World. There is so much love for me from Justin and my "dearest friend." **Love and more love. xoxo**

I could validate each message from Justin, my "dearest friend" and Scott. However, there are other compelling stories we would like to share with you.

The Spirit World decides we should move on to the next chapter.

Namaste.

Travel enriches your mind, relaxes your body, and rejuvenates your soul.

– Cheryl Kay

SPIRIT SOUL CONNECTIONS

15 February 2020

Travelling abroad with my Spirit friends is easy – there are no weight restrictions on their luggage; they don't need to take any!

Bags packed, I'm off on another Earth Soul rejuvenation retreat and adventure. This journey, I'm travelling to spiritually blessed Siem Reap in Cambodia. On this trip, I intend to leave my ego at home. I aim to relax and reconnect with my Earth Soul, including my Spirit Soul family and friends.

The most exciting time for me is when I travel overseas to places of simplicity. My ability to connect with the Spirit World on these trips is effortless. The veil between the Earth's atmosphere and the Spirit World is at its most delicate, resembling sheer beautiful silk that flows elegantly in the breeze. The connections, conversations and alignments I experience during my travels are fantastic memories to have. My ability to hear, see and feel Spirit's presence is sensational during this time.

Following their guidance is natural; listening to them is easy. Without distractions, our time together is uninterrupted. Their messages make me smile and laugh. Thinking of some moments and memories, I need tissues after a flood of tears.

I always feel happy when I get to spend quality time with the Spirit World. They always shower me with love and serenity. The Spirit World and I have a great passion for sharing and showing others how easy it is to communicate with each other.

*We don't say goodbye and neither do they.
Instead, we say, "See you later!"*

xoxo

Spirit Souls make great travel companions. On one overseas trip to the city of Siem Reap in Cambodia, I experienced several inspiring connections with the Spirit World. The first prominent experience occurred on the second morning of my stay. I had woken up just before 7am to go for a swim in the hotel pool before having my breakfast. I looked at the pool area from my

The veil between the Earth atmosphere and the Spirit world is delicate, resembling sheer beautiful silk that flows elegantly in the breeze.

balcony to discover the staff vacuuming the pool. I checked my watch; it was 6:55am and the cleaner was only two-thirds of the way through cleaning. The opening time of 7am was not viable. Being my usual Earth Soul self, I felt the stir of frustration rise in me. Several minutes passed, then the Spirit World interrupted my internal whining with clear guidance and clarity. ***"Choose a different route. You don't need to do the same thing every day."*** Their message was short, sharp and to the point. Before my restless mind could interfere in our conversation, I took their advice and went for a walk.

During this time, memorable messages began to flow to me from the Spirit World. I could feel the gentle pull of their energy as they guided me around the streets of Siem Reap, pointing out landmarks I had been thinking of finding. There were no words to express their presence. It was a surreal experience. The warmth of their energy stayed with me for the remainder of that day. It was awesome, wandering the streets of Siem Reap with my Spirit family and friends.

I love connecting with the Spirit World. I encourage others to do the same.

Those in the Spirit World love you without judgement. They're there to help us discover solutions to situations that are part of our learning here in the Earth's atmosphere. Remember, they've experienced our dense gloomy atmosphere and they have an abundance of wisdom. They continue to love and empower us eternally, extending the hand of friendship to us without any conditions attached.

Another great attribute of the Spirit World is their awareness of our internal thoughts, along with the battles we experience as physical Earth Souls living in the Earth realm. While we are processing our thoughts and thinking, they're already using their energy to reach out to us, offering guidance and solutions. Being wired continuously to the technology of our physical world, we often miss or ignore their signposts of guidance.

Our connection to the Spirit World can be as simple as a loving thought.

When you get an opportunity, take a moment out of your day to send lovely messages to a family member or friend in Spirit. They will be happy to hear from you.

Once you become comfortable with this method, then you may feel more empowered to speak your thoughts or messages out loud to them.

Either way, whether you think or speak, the Spirit Soul family will be happy to hear from you.

Further along in our book, we have documented some communication styles for you to browse through. These may give you an idea of a style that suits your personality.

The bond between my loved ones in the Spirit World and myself has grown stronger since their transitions. I love them; they love me back every day. With their guidance and their validations, they have a splendid view from the Spirit World of my daily life in the Earth's atmosphere.

Through my eyes, this is how we might interpret Spirit World messages:

When we enter the Earth's atmosphere as physical Earth Souls, we have signed a contract to attend Earth Soul school. We're here on individual contracts to learn, live and evolve. We do eventually return to our Spirit Soul home to test the lessons and experiences of our physical Earth Soul's journey. Our comfortable Spiritual home provides a remarkable atmosphere that allows us to travel between the two realms using our energy.

The Spirit World often tells me they love working with their memories. They get to revisit and relive beautiful experiences they've shared with family and friends still living in Earth Soul school.

> **We don't say goodbye and neither do they. Instead, we say, "See you later!"**
>
> **xoxo**

Spirit whispered, "Keep listening with your pen poised, ready to write." You are in safe hands when the Spirit world calls.

– Cheryl Kay

SPIRITS SPEAKING TO ME

A Spirit named Lilly

26 March 2019
A Spirit wakes me up, tells me her name is Lilly.

27 March 2019
Lilly wakes me up, tells me she's visiting again.

28 March 2019
While out driving, I pass a car with the number plates LILLY. Lilly then informs me she is in my car with me and did I like how she got my attention. I love her ingenuity. I am still trying to figure out who Lilly is and why I have become her focus. I wonder if she might be one of my Spirit guides. Driving and talking to Spirits is awkward. I mention subtly we might enjoy the journey together and resume our communication once I reach my destination.

29 March 2019
In the middle of the night, I wake up to another visit from Lilly. I go out to my kitchen to discover the beautiful perfume of roses.

Lilly explains to me how much she loves roses. The perfume smell is so exquisite. I linger in the kitchen for several minutes, taking in the magic of the Spirit Realm.

30 March 2019

Lilly wakes me in the early hours of the morning to show me a house on stilts and the word "Queenslander" is echoing in my ears.

Lilly shows me fresh dirt underneath the house.

Lilly shows me a man and a woman. The man is in front, the lady is to the side of him.

Lilly shows me a flip case – a cigarette case – cherry red in colour with gold lettering on it reading "DUNHILL."

The next morning, I finally ask my husband if he has a relative by the name of Lilly.

He says yes, so I go ahead and explain to him that Lilly has been visiting from the Spirit World.

The narrative between us goes something like this. I get straight to the point, just like Lilly. I reveal the following to him:

Lilly loves roses; she smoked Dunhill cigarettes. Lilly also described her home to me; it was a Queenslander-style home. For some odd reason, she feels compelled to show me something under the house while proclaiming emphatically, "A very bossy man."

My husband's reply is swift and to the point. "Lilly was my mother's sister-in-law. She loved roses and had an extensive rose garden. She lived in a house like you described, and yes, her husband was bossy. He would bang on the table when he

wanted something brought to him. Each day when he arrived home from work, he would sound the car horn. Lilly would have to run down and open the garage door, so he didn't have to get out of the car and do it himself."

I think out loud, "Holy crap! That is appalling. That is terrible. What the…!"

My husband's next question is: "Why is she visiting? Also, you're freaking me out with your spooky stuff!"

Hubby's last statement doesn't deter me; I patiently explain that I believe he must have had a special bond with Lilly when she was an Earth Soul. "Lilly is reaching out to you, possibly, with some important news coming your way."

My husband looks at me, "Yer, yer, yer, okay."

A Spirit named Denise

25 September 2019

Denise communicates, "My brother Gordon has arrived home."

This detailed transcript is the connection/conversation I experienced with Denise's Spirit Soul.

Denise: *"I had been sitting with Gordon for a few weeks, patiently waiting for the go-ahead from him to come home to his Spiritual home."*

Denise tells me they have a lot of catching up to do.

I sense Denise smiling a big smile. I feel a sense of immense happiness; a beautiful warmth washes over me, a very soothing energy.

Denise shows me an event that occurred when she and Gordon were living in the Earth's atmosphere as brother and sister. Denise fell pregnant out of wedlock. Her parents removed the baby from her arms. Strangers came to the family home to collect her newborn. Gordon tried to stop the inevitable happening, unsuccessfully. He then watched as his sister sat drowning in her tears.

Denise affirms that Gordon was the only person who ever stuck up for her during her past life in the Earth's atmosphere.

Denise then abruptly changes the topic. This time she illustrates the name Lillian.

Denise continues: **"Lillian, Gordon and I share a connection from our previous life in the Earth's atmosphere."**

What is the connection between these three Spirit Souls?

Lillian is the Spirit Soul who had regularly visited me before. An experienced Spirit Soul when interacting with me, she was bright with her energy. The way she communicated was effortless and easy for me to interpret.

It turns out Denise is my husband's mother. She transitioned some years ago, after a culmination of sadness that started with the frightful removal of her firstborn child. The following years also brought her painful physical life experiences regularly.

I need to mention I had not met Lillian or Denise physically before they visited me as Spirit Souls. I had the pleasure of meeting Gordon occasionally on this side of life. The most memorable time was at lunch on his 70th birthday.

The Spirit Realm had made me aware of his pending journey home. Denise had regularly communicated with me, often through the smell of cigarettes she loved to smoke. Her connection and messages intensified as the time drew closer. She was looking forward to her brother's arrival.

With a lot of finesse, I quizzed my husband for answers. Denise and Gordon were brother and sister, and Lillian was Denise's sister-in-law. With certain parts of the jigsaw completed, it was easy to recognise future messages from the three of them.

Denise and Lillian enjoy a lovely friendship in the Spirit World. They shared similar experiences as Earth Souls. When Lillian arrived in the Spirit World, Denise was there to greet her. Denise often shows me a vision of the two of them, strolling side by side – a picture-perfect postcard from the Spirit World.

A Spirit named Guinevere

Guinevere and I share an empathetic conversation as she interacts with me. She is a Spirit Soul that I felt had not fully transitioned after suffering a traumatic departure from the Earth's atmosphere.

Here is a description of my interaction with Guinevere, showing the way we communicate and interpret a Spirit Soul's message.

Guinevere presents herself to me as a young teenager.

She is wearing a T-shirt and bone-coloured shorts. The pockets are unusual as they hang below the hemline of her shorts.

Guinevere tells me, "*I don't want to be here. Why am I here?*"

Guinevere shows me a building with a sloping grassed area covered in snow. She wants to be back there.

Guinevere is describing her school. The grassed area covered with snow represents her love of ice skating and skiing.

After her traumatic departure, Guinevere's Soul continued to hover around the places where she felt connected and safe. The school and the ice-skating arenas were two of these places.

Guinevere also shows me a high, black-coloured fence.

*

Guinevere continued describing her school to me. I visited the school with another Medium to offer Guinevere guidance and help her understand the benefits of her completing her transition.

When I visited the school, I immediately noticed the fence. It was high and green, not black as Guinevere had described. It wasn't until I looked at the fencing from inside the school grounds that I noticed the colour was no longer green; it was black.

It was then I realised the importance of her message. She was validating that inside the school ground, was her realm of safety and she saw outside through the black fence line. I could now decipher her message accurately.

Guinevere's brother Jacob had already completed his transition through to the light and had returned home to the Spirit World. He waited patiently for his sister, who was halfway

between realms. He wanted her to complete her transition, though he also understood her decision not to complete the journey. Guinevere stayed because she was trying to console her mother.

Jacob confided in me, openly expressing that he had become tired of being afraid while living his physical life. Jacob showed me how he had tried to protect his sister right up to the end of their physical Earth Soul lives.

Jacob said that, after their father had murdered both him and his sister, *"I travelled back to my Spirit home, relieved to be free from the fearful Earth Soul life I had endured."*

Helping Guinevere

There is a ceremony we've created to assist Souls who haven't completed their transition.

When a Spirit reaches out to us for help or support, we as Mediums validate and create a safe environment for these Souls to transition.

It is important to highlight we do not force a Soul to go through to the light. Instead, we assist with their decision and the journey. We act as confidantes.

In the transition cases in this book, there have been two other experienced Mediums, Judy and Cathie. Together the three of us love being of service to the Spirit Realm. We have created our personalised transition ceremony.

To assist Guinevere, we decided to hold the ceremony in July of 2018, close to the school she had attended because in reaching out to me, she had made the school a big focal point.

As we set out our crystals, we felt Guinevere's energy. We listened, feeling Guinevere's energy, and communicated with her as a Medium does.

Guinevere's brother Jacob – his Spirit energy – arrived, very excited at the prospect that his sister might join him in the Spirit World at last.

Jacob was extending his Spirit Soul energy out to Guinevere, reaching out to take her gently by the hand; a very emotional moment between them.

Guinevere had been staying close to the Earth's atmosphere to avoid meeting her father again. Her father had ended his Earth Soul life hours after he had ended theirs.

We explain to Guinevere that in the Spirit World, she won't have any connection to, or with her father. We assure Guinevere she will be on a higher vibration than her father. His efforts to reunite himself with his children via death will not eventuate.

We felt we were making some progress.

Guinevere speaks: *"I have a message for him: I'm not like you; all for nothing. We will not reunite in the Spirit World. Your energy is no longer attached to mine. I am now free of you."*

Guinevere expresses she is sorry. *"For a moment I forgot Mum's advice; I let my guard down. I opened the door."* Guinevere is also hesitant; she doesn't want to leave her

mum. We explain to Guinevere that communicating with her mum will be easier once she has gone through to the light, to her Spiritual home.

Guinevere speaks: ***"I miss my mum." xoxo***

Judy, Cathie and I continued to help Guinevere lovingly, gently, patiently. We waited for her decision on whether she would take the last leg of her journey home to her Spirit home where her Spirit Soul now belonged.

We continued to support and stay with her. It was such a beautiful moment when Guinevere's Spirit Soul took one last look at the school. With her beloved schoolbooks under her ethereal wings, her energy moved away from us slowly. She stopped for a moment, looked back at the three of us, then she held out her hand for her brother Jacob to guide her on her last leg of her journey, back to the Spirit World.

Guinevere speaks: ***"I'm leaving your world. I'm going home."***

The three of us were very emotional – such a lovely young Earth Soul with a big, beautiful smile.

We look forward to her Spirit Soul visits.

From the Spirit World, Guinevere reconnected with me days later, showing me her Spirit Soul sprinkling precious energy around her mum's broken heart.

In December 2018, Guinevere's mum's Earth Soul transitioned back to the Spirit World to be with her children. The day before her transition, I kept hearing a common surname repeatedly. The next day I read in the newspaper that Guinevere

and Jacob's mum had departed her Earth Soul life at her home. Hearing this name was validation from the Spirit World that Guinevere and Jacob's mum was in the process of an early transition to reunite with her children.

A Spirit Soul on the overbridge

11 December 2018

I was on a train travelling from the Central Coast going to Sydney. We had just passed through Eastwood station, and as we neared an overhead bridge, a young man jumped straight in front of our approaching train. The young man exited the Earth's atmosphere right before my eyes. His Soul Spirit saw my reaction and heard my question: "What happened to you on the Earth's plane that made you want to leave early?"

I must admit I was a little shocked when his Spirit Soul sat next to me and proceeded to answer my questions. First, he showed me how a calmness had washed over him just before he had jumped. He then described how he had felt rejected in the Earth's atmosphere, unequivocally stating he had just wanted to go back to his Spiritual home. I then asked him his name. It took me a few goes to work it out and understand his translation. His name was Billy. Being inquisitive, I asked Billy, "So where is home?"

Without hesitation, ***"The Spirit World,"*** was his reply. Next question!

He gazed at my shocked facial expression. I responded just as swiftly, "Hey Billy, I talk to dead people all the time. I just

didn't expect to be communicating with someone so quickly, so soon after their transition."

His reply was poignant: *"I didn't expect to be meeting you, the Medium, today either."*

Billy and I continued to correspond. At one point, he showed me a pear and a spinning top. (My Medium interpretation was that it all went pear-shaped for him – a downward spiral of sorts at spinning-top speed.) Billy felt that no one had noticed his physical mind struggles; a feeling of insignificance had permanently swept over him. His parting words were, *"Hey, I wasn't on anyone's radar."*

Before I could ask Billy what he meant, I felt his energy disconnecting. Tears were flowing down my cheeks.

To my surprise, I felt his energy return briefly. He expressed, with gratitude, *"Thank you for connecting with me. Also, thank you for caring. As I now approach the light to complete my transition home, the warmth and compassion you showed to me as a total stranger is a gift I will carry with me to my Soul's home."*

The young man, Billy, has left a lasting impression on me emotionally. Our meeting resembled a sliding doors moment. Spiritually, we passed each other in a corridor between the Earth's atmosphere and the Spirit World.

Billy, a young man with blond hair and beautiful blue eyes, transitioned through the tunnel of illuminated light. Billy's energy became a lightning bolt as he headed toward his Spiritual home.

Spirits communicate with us in ways we do not understand. In our physical world, we associate through what we can physically see. Sadly, our society has conditioned us to ignore those subtle feelings and bumps in the night or day – connections that come from the Spirit World.

Can I suggest you pause for a minute and send some love to someone you know in the Spirit World? They will be ecstatic – beyond joyful. Be part of the revolution!

***We don't say goodbye and neither do they.
Instead, we say, "See you later!"***

xoxo

After/life a return to wholeness of our Spirit Soul.

A Spirit seeks my help

2 January 2019

A young man.

    Jet-black wavy hair.

    A teenager.

    He sits next to me. He's a Spirit Soul seeking help.

    He describes to me how he had two more jobs to do.

    He shows himself walking downstairs towards a dungeon (cellar). The word "dungeon" has a distinct echo to it.

    He then feels compelled to be more vivid as he describes the staircase leading down towards the dungeon (cellar): wide steps, a steep descent. The staircase narrows in width as you walk down it.

    He shows me the back view of his body as he walks down the stairs, with an emphasis on what he is wearing – it's a particular style of clothing.

    The clothing is white.

    The back part of the clothing has a distinctive square panel with light-blue detail.

    The young man is adamant that I note the pale small blue stripe.

    He tells me he transitioned early after the last two jobs. He had no choices left; he was owned by men of influence. He was handed around to men of influence for their sexual gratification. He feared and was convinced that no one would believe his story. "Entrapment" was the word he showed me.

"Please, can you help me?"

I enquire about him not completing his transition.

He states that he wants to stop these men from hurting others; he has unfinished business.

I then explain that his Soul needs to transition completely. Hovering and trying to exist between realms will not help his Soul or produce positive outcomes, or stop the cruelty perpetrated by the individuals. I gently explain to him he no longer belongs here in the Earth's atmosphere and that his Soul can achieve much more once he completes his transition.

The young man then makes three statements:

"He is guilty."

"Simon says."

"Stew-art."

I recommend that he consider my option and that I will happily assist him.

Judy, Cathie and I regularly hold these *assisted transition* ceremonies. Together the three of us facilitate a unique transition service for this young man.

Now that he is safely home, he has connected with me to validate his newfound freedom. He is using his Spirit energy with outstanding success to assist others who are healing from similar experiences. There has been considerable unearthing of evidence surrounding sexual abuse that occurred by church leaders and their associates, involving this teenager and others.

*

Sometimes when a Soul seeks our help, it can be a very emotional experience for us. Often these Souls have endured pain and cruelty beyond our comprehension. It can be very frightening and confronting when they describe or share details of their experiences. It's not uncommon for the Medium/s to require several days of rest after an **assisted transition**. You may feel emotionally depleted and mentally exhausted after the event, especially if the Soul's physical life ended in violence or tragedy.

Assisted transitions can also be quirky, cheerful occasions. Some Spirit Souls delay their journey through to the light for a variety of different reasons. An example of this is my next encounter with a Spirit Soul who had a band play music in my right ear, at loud decibels. This Spirit Soul was flamboyant and not in the least bit shy about introducing himself.

"Hi. My name is Freddie."

Freddie transitioned early. He had been experiencing a successful comeback in the music industry. He decided he would try to flout universal laws by existing between the two worlds.

Freddie communicated how, while living in the Earth's atmosphere, he had been creative and had lived by his own rules. He loved living an adrenalin-fuelled life, frequently crossing boundaries, stretching friendships and flaunting his sexuality. His lifestyle ultimately caught up with him. Medically diagnosed with a terminal health issue, Freddie endured a *gradual transition* from the Earth's atmosphere.

After multiple communications and deliberations, Freddie finally agreed that a full transition to the Spirit World would be more beneficial for his Spirit Soul.

The ability to be creative in the Spirit World would assure his contentment. He could also still stay connected to family, friends and the music industry that he loved so much here in the Earth's atmosphere.

"Can I continue to validate and communicate through music?"

"Yes, Freddie."

In keeping with Freddie's entertainer personality, we decided his **assisted transition** through to the light would be a celebration. Judy, the Master of Ceremonies for the event, purchased champagne. She also wrote an excellent tribute letter to Freddie. Cathie's opening and closing ceremony using her sacred ritual were light-hearted – poignant for Freddie's personality. I kept the line of communication open to Freddie. He was beside himself with joy, especially when we started singing his favourite songs. The mood and atmosphere were lively. After two hours of music and dance, a bright light wrapped its energy around Freddie. It looked like he was going on stage to perform a concert. I could see his signature smile beaming. An army of Spirit Souls greeted him as he danced his way to the light into the arms of a multitude of Spirit World music fans.

"Au revoir (goodbye) Freddie, belle âme (beautiful Soul)."

Freddie stays in touch. The date of his **assisted transition** was 7 November 2018.

Freddie is one of my regular visiting Spirit friends. His energy is like a breath of fresh air that drifts in and out of my life.

Sometimes Freddie will do the most random things to get my attention. In the early hours of one particular morning, I was driving home from work when I looked in my car rear-vision mirror to find Freddie smiling at me. Then when I looked back at the road, a car in front of me had the number plate FR34ED. On this occasion, Freddie freaked me out. I soon recovered, then I just laughed. Typical Freddie style.

I cherish our ongoing friendship. Lifestyle choices and social acceptance in the Earth's atmosphere have changed a lot since Freddie's Earth Soul transitioned home. Freddie appraises the current Earth's atmosphere. ***"If I were an Earth Soul today, I could rock the world."*** Yes, Freddie, I know!

A Spirit Soul named Rose

Indignity.

When Rose's Spirit Soul first contacted me, the first word I heard was "INDIGNITY," emphatically spoken.

Rose expressed herself about the feelings, disrespect and disregard that her husband had shown her and felt towards her. He was not at all concerned about his appalling treatment of her.

Rose tells me she was aware of his indiscretions. He flaunted his behaviour in front of her as a constant reminder that her presence revolted him. She never imagined that he would kill her to have the life he wanted. His ego was enormous!

Rose reiterates her feelings of being manipulated and insignificant.

Rose didn't complete her transition, choosing instead to stay close to the Earth's atmosphere. Adamant that she wants him

brought to justice, she wants everyone to know the truth. She wants her children to know she didn't leave them voluntarily.

As a Medium, I love being of service to the Spirit World. In Rose's case, I wanted to encourage her to complete her transition – to go through to the light, to her Spirit Soul home. There she would find peace and learn a new technique to communicate effectively and affectionately with her children still in the Earth's atmosphere.

The healing she would receive would help replace her current energy with a new ethereal energy that would enable her to communicate with her children effortlessly.

It took some gentle persuading and coaxing. Eventually, Rose opened the door and stepped into the light of her Spiritual home.

Judy, Cathie and I felt the energy shift as Rose parted ways with us. A few days later, Rose's Spirit Soul came to visit me. Her energy felt different this time; her aura was calm, confident and serene. Her dignity was restored.

Rose worked with her newfound Spirit energy, eventually getting her murder case noticed by the powers that be in the Earth's atmosphere. They have charged her husband with her murder; he is awaiting trial.

Rose assured me she will be in attendance during his murder trial. Confidently, she announced, ***"Once in the courtroom, you can expect my presence. I'll continually encompass my children with love. Let the truth provide the clarity they deserve. My husband may not see me at his trial, though he will feel me!"***

Young Spirit Souls speak

A group of young children interact with me. They were seeking help to find their teacher so they could all complete transition together.

They were very visual in their communication. The best way to document this connection was to write and sketch all the details as they showed them to me.

The visual aspects of our communication, their attention to detail was incredible.

These were a group of young children, aged between 6 and 10 years of age. They were all sitting in a row in a building with glass windows. Some appeared to be sitting at desks all facing out, looking out, while others had their little faces pressed up against the window. They were all wearing white shirts with soft pale-blue vests. They all had blond-coloured hair. The description of the room was precise.

Further research revealed that this group of children had not completed their transition home to the Spirit World. They wanted to reconnect with their teacher who had become displaced from them.

I spoke to the children, detailing the benefits of completing their transition, promising to ask for help with locating their beloved teacher. It became apparent that these children were remarkably close to their teacher; they said they were fond of her, adding that they also had great trust in her.

I asked the Spirit World for some guidance. Almost instantly, an adolescent female with long black hair stepped forward. She

was wearing a red ochre coloured tunic-style dress. Her energy was colourful and vibrant. It was easy to see why the children were so fond of her.

The children were ecstatic to see her. She hugged them all individually before asking them to form a line and hold on to the hand of the person next to them. She sang beautifully in Russian, **"We are going for a magic carpet ride in the clouds."** One of the little boys didn't want to hold hands. He said his name was Viktor. He eventually followed the others, still refusing to hold onto a classmate's hand.

I became emotional during this assisted transition. The events that had unfolded during the massacre of these children and their teacher have lingered with me.

Dear Earth soul
As you ascend your staircase of life, don't forget to pause momentarily along the way – to take in the view, to reflect on your progress, and to honour your Earth soul's growth along the way.

– Team Spirit

A powerful quote has the potential to transform the energy of your Earth soul's life. Namaste.

– Cheryl Kay

SPIRIT SPEAKS

Quotes from the Spirit World

Spirit speaks

"One life experience at a time, a transition and re-entry take place. The life you live here in the Earth's atmosphere is one life as an Earth Soul. You return to the Spirit World as a Spirit Soul after your physical Earth life. When we incarnate/evolve, it is a new life, new experiences, new lessons. We are all the same, regardless of faith, religion, culture."

Spirit speaks

"Completing our experiences in the Earth's atmosphere as Earth Souls, we shed our physical bodies and return to our Spiritual home as ethereal Spirit Souls."

Spirit speaks

"Sprinkle fairy dust wherever you go in the Earth's atmosphere, not bullshit. Fairy dust is the manifestation

of magic into your human life experiences. Bullshit only leaves a permanent stain on whoever and wherever it lands!"

Spirit speaks

"In our Spiritual home, the Spirit World is inclusive; all religions, all faiths, all cultures. We are one."

Spirit speaks

"Our energy will always stay connected to you. We stay connected because we love you. xoxo."

Spirit speaks

"Replacing my physical presence with my Soul presence took some time for me after I transitioned home. It's been worth it. Now every day I get to spend time with you. Connecting my energy to yours is easy for me from my Spirit Soul home. Better than Wi-Fi internet. Quicker too!"

Spirit speaks

"D-E-A-T-H.

Depart Earth's Atmosphere Transition Home (to our Spiritual home).

We relinquish our physical bodies back to Mother Nature. Then our Soul returns home to our Spiritual family."

My precious gift for my Earth Soul mum is eternal love, mummy I visit you everyday Love more Love. xoxo.

Spirit speaks

"Our language is unique; we communicate with you using a variety of signs, symbols, energy and even charades! You will need to think outside the square when you communicate with us. Be creative; we appreciate it."

Spirit Speaks

"Dear Earth Soul, faith and courage go hand in hand. Having faith gives you courage!"

Spirit speaks

"After your contract reaches completion, you shed your physical Earth Soul body and return to your

Spiritual home in the form of delicate, light ethereal energy."

Spirit speaks

"Our comfortable Spiritual home provides remarkable experiences for us. Using our delightful ethereal Soul Spirit energy, we visit your Earth's atmosphere regularly, bringing gifts of love and healing."

Spirit speaks

"On a subconscious level, my Earth Soul realised its departure time from the Earth's atmosphere. Family and friends were openly exclaiming that my departure was sudden and unexpected. My other family and friends in the Spirit World disagreed. Our energy in the Spirit World vibrates at a frequency not available in the Earth's atmosphere. The saying we are light years away is real. xoxo."

Spirit speaks

"Life/Afterlife is without borders or boundaries."

Spirit speaks

"My Soul transitioned at a young age.

"I shared a precious legacy with my Earth Soul family. My gift to them was eternal love.

"When I left so young, so early, the family I left behind could not comprehend my departure. They

were inconsolable with grief. I continued to send love to them. Over time they adjusted to loving me without my physical body.

"It was not until they had lived through their grief that the purpose of my short time with them became more evident: long-lasting love.

"I am now an evolved Soul from the highest Realm in the Spirit heavens.

"I continue to send messages of love to my Earth Soul family; this I will continue until their Souls complete their Earth Soul cycle. There is no comparison between emotional love and guidance or material wealth. Ask any parent who has a child transition home early. They learn to live without them physically, though emotionally, the bond grows stronger."

> We don't say goodbye and neither do they.
> Instead, we say, "See you later!"
> Love and more love. xoxo

The Spirit realm's advice: "Communication with us takes place when you give your Earth soul creative licence."

– Cheryl Kay

LIFE/AFTERLIFE

What happens the moment after you die? I put this enquiry out to the Spirit World.

My spirit soul walks with you every day remember I'm only ever a heartbeat away, Love more Love.

Spirit speaks

"There is a sense of lingering. The Soul pauses before transitioning to take a last look at life in the physical world. The Soul now understands that the physical body has become just a shell, and the energy contained will transcend back to being their Spirit Soul, not a physical Earth Soul."

Spirit speaks

"We would like to recommend to family, friends and hospice staff of palliative patients, that they try a fresh approach for these Earth Souls who are experiencing gradual departures. Remove the clinical atmosphere approach and replace it with a Spiritually blessed feeling. The immediate moment after their death should be respected, and the moment of their transition honoured. The Soul lingers before the moment of transition – the last look at life in the physical world."

The Spirit's communication intrigued me as I delved further and asked for more detail. They have said that it would be more beneficial for family and friends to remove the clinical atmosphere of the room. Instead, it would be lovely to furnish the room so that it is pleasing to the eye – add a touch of beautiful fresh flowers, play favourite music, have the family reminisce over past

times and honour them before they transition. Families who can put their own grief aside make for a fitting farewell.

Immediately after the prana has left the body, celebrate their transition.

I know I would personally love scattered rose petals – a lasting impression for any Soul to take with them on their journey home.

Does inspired thought reveal that it's time for a performance review?

– Cheryl Kay

SPIRIT GENERAL MEETING

Justin and my "dearest friend" – their Spirit Souls – come breezing into my lounge room together. Their energy tells me they're excited. Together they declare, "The Spirit World has called a general meeting; they want to hold it in your lounge room."

WOW! I'm curious, nervous and excited all at once. An unfamiliar experience is unfolding for me. Justin and my "dearest friend" assure me I'm up for the task and offer their help as my mind goes into overdrive. "What time? What day? Blah blah blah," I babble.

Their signature smiles bring me back to Earth's atmosphere. Their gentle descriptive message to me is, **"All's good; trust your intuition. We'll be back to help. We love you."** *xoxo*

I visualise creating a perfect atmosphere for the pending meeting. I mentally make notes on how I would like the room to look and feel for the event: Beautiful, colourful flowers; a white bunch of roses for Justin and a purple bunch of roses for my "dearest friend"; crystals to enhance the room's energy, music to raise the vibration and incense to clear the room of any lingering negative energy.

I remind myself to prepare and organise my accompanying invocations. Maybe I could write something special for the occasion.

I have received many physical precious gifts from the Spirit World, such as feathers and coins. These will also add that perfect feel to the room for this extraordinary event.

Leading up to our meeting, the Spirit World and I have enjoyed crystal clear communication as we were in sync with each other. My ability to understand and interpret their messages has increased tenfold.

Sixty plus years have passed. Still, some people concede that in their minds I'm weird. I appreciate my journey of self-discovery and my role as being of service to the Spirit World. I feel there has been a shift of consciousness where Earth Souls are now relating to, and seeking to understand **Life/Afterlife**. I continue to enjoy the tremendous satisfaction I get when I am on my high-flying disc, aligning with my Spirit World family.

We are all Souls existing on different levels of Spiritual maturity and evolvement.

In our physical world, when we think of a business general meeting, we envisage an ego-driven event. Players jostle for better positions within the structure. Other players become collateral damage, null and void. Changes can occur in systems that are not always of the highest order or necessity.

In the Spirit World, I discovered their general meetings focused on healing, encouragement, acknowledgement, and a lot of love, with a little humour thrown into the mix. Their yin-yang

balance was refreshingly delightful. There was no ego attached to any of the attendees' Spirit Souls, Ascended Masters or Spirit guides. The energy of this room was one of happiness. You could feel their presence, their love and the right to communicate openly and honestly.

When I reminisce about this event, I experience a rush of warm feelings. Yes, many, many beautiful healings took place at our general meeting. My life changed; an alignment took place. The Spirit World presented me with a new portfolio, ESM (Earth Soul Mentor), which involves providing guidance and leadership in the areas of communication and validation of Life/Afterlife.

"We want you to reach out to anyone who needs help to communicate. Teach the Earth Souls how to talk to us, sing to us or write us a letter, as we can read it as they write! We just want to be part of their everyday life; we love them, with no strings attached."

Their guidance was profound, and I felt their pure love.

"There will be multiple avenues for you to explore to become a successful educator. Trust us, trust yourself and trust your intuition."

For several hours after our gathering, I reflected upon the connection, the communication. It was exciting. We had created an opportunity together to teach Earth Souls how to interpret their messages from family and friends who have transitioned home to the Spirit World.

> *We don't say goodbye and neither do they.*
> *Instead, we say, "See you later!"*
>
> *xoxo*

Throughout this book, we've endeavoured to offer ways to help Earth Souls discover their unique voice when communicating with their family and friends who have transitioned home.

We sincerely encourage you to develop your own signature communication style, signs and signals, with an emphasis on **"We are one; we just live in different realms."**

I look forward to continuing the ceremony to the light-assisted transitions. I'm very enthusiastic about receiving visitations from these Spirit Souls. They're some of my best teachers. This way, I get to learn and teach respectively. Wow, what a fulfilling perfect vocation and way of life for me. I'm ecstatic, happy.

Namaste.

*When your Earth soul seeks validation, meditation
and reflection holds the key!*

– Cheryl Kay

AFTERWORD

Dear Earth Soul

A Spirited letter from the Spirit Realm to you, the reader. The Spirit World is overjoyed with your aspiring to be part of our revolution.

> **We don't say goodbye and neither do they.**
> **Instead, we say, "See you later!"**
>
> *xoxo*

Dear Earth Soul,

We're so glad you have chosen our book to expand on your ability to connect with us in the Spirit World. We applaud your courage to go against the Earth atmosphere's current trend of "seeing is believing."

We love your "Aha" moments when your physical Earth Soul thoughts align perfectly with our message to you. Communicate, validate; that's how we rock 'n' roll with you!

Don't doubt your ability; you're a beautiful, bright, creative Soul making remarkable inroads into communicating with us Spirit energy Souls.

Namaste. We love you. xoxo

"Spirit's door is always open." Give them a shoutout, Say Hi!

– Cheryl Kay

TO BE CONTINUED …

A new book is coming …

"The Transcript Mode" is currently in the initial stages of a first draft.

When Earth Souls return to their Spiritual home, a celebration awaits them. They attend a majestic event, the *Afterparty*, held in their honour to celebrate their transition from the Earth's atmosphere – a manifestation of my belief in "Life/Afterlife." During this momentous occasion, they lovingly share stories of their experiences as Earth Souls.

Looking from their panoramic viewpoint, they pledge to continue to offer physical Earth Souls' family and friends resounding guidance.

But wait, there's more!

A beautiful burst of Spirit energy comes gliding into my lounge room.

"Just as love is eternal, so is our connection to your physical world. We are a new tribe of transitioned souls, having fun at our *Afterparty*, celebrating our return to our Spiritual home. We made commitments to family and friends in the Earth's atmosphere before we transitioned to reach out and communicate regularly. Communication with the Spirit World is now considered funky. A revolution is in the making!"

> **We don't say goodbye, and neither do they.**
> **Instead, we say, "See you later!"**
>
> ***xoxo***

*I believe in Inspired thought, bumps in the night!
Intuition and mystical magic "Spiritology"*

– Cheryl Kay

CHERYL KAY – SPIRITOLOGY

Assisted transition: A Spirit Soul seeks help from a Psychic Medium to help them complete their journey home.

Ceremony: An event that the Spirit World acknowledges to assist a Soul seeking help to complete their transition.

Crystal grid: Intuitively selecting crystals to form the personal framework for the Soul seeking assistance.

Earth Soul: Our physical self/Soul. Attendees of Earth school.

Ethereal energy: Astral energy that the Spirit Souls use when they're communicating with us in the Earth's atmosphere.

Invocation: Connecting to specialists in the Spirit World seeking help to create a refined atmosphere for the scheduled assisted transition.

Opening and closing ceremony: Sacred rituals to create a sanctum for the transitions.

Prana: Life force or vital energy. Our vital breath. We are universal energy that flows in and around the body.

Spirit Soul: Our non-physical self/Soul. Immortal.

The light: The portal of view that the Earth Soul enters through when leaving the physical Earth's atmosphere.

Transition: When the Earth Soul's Spirit leaves their physical body. The conclusion of the physical life experience.

Namaste: When souls greet each other with "Namaste", a ring of spiritual emotion is created. This connection can be from either side of the Life/Afterlife veil. The salutation Namaste creates a circle of bliss, passing positive energy onto the one receiving the gesture. The heart chakras are also known to connect during the divine expression of Hello; the love and light within me acknowledges the love and light within you.

Life/Afterlife: We are all Eternal souls who continue to evolve by way of living Life after Life. We come into the physical world each time with a blueprint plan to experience a new physical life and learn physical life lessons. On completion of this experience, we then transition back to the Spirit realm as a Spirit soul. There we continue to live in a different form without the physical body "ethereal energy". The Spirit world is where our highest guidance is offered. We evaluate and evolve; soul growth. The energy in the Spirit world is full of light colourful in comparison to the Earth atmosphere where the energy is dense. Two very different lives our souls' live.

How do you assist unsettled souls?
Be a friend, listen without infringing.
Respect and cherish that it is their journey, not yours!

– Cheryl Kay

MASTER OF CEREMONIES, CANDLES, WHITE SAGE AND ILLUMINATION

The venue

When a Spirit Soul reaches out for help, a process is undertaken to establish their needs. We telepathically connect and discuss what action is required: *"How can I be of service?"* Their story enables me to begin the process I call **Ceremony to the Light**.

When the Soul agrees to transition, intuitively we find a suitable venue. Sometimes the Spirit Soul only wants to cross over and is not concerned with these details. However, it is an honour for me when the Spirit asks me to choose the venue on their behalf.

Over the past three years the most remarkable venues have been at a school, McDonalds, Shelly Beach, Toowoon Bay and at the home of a generous colleague of mine. Judy is also a master at venue preparation.

In some circumstances where the Earth Soul has departed under horrific circumstances, we need to take a gentle and

sensitive approach. During assisted transitions, emotions can be heightened, so we may choose to utilise the privacy of our own homes. This allows us to communicate and comfort them in a more composed environment. Preparation of the venue allows the Medium to tap into the lifestyle of the Spirit Soul, pre-departure.

Examples
1) An entertainer: We chose a party theme with music, singing, dancing and champagne.
2) A mother who had been murdered by her husband: She wanted her children to know the truth. Utilising Judy's expertise, we held her assisted transition at Judy's home. She transformed her living room into an atmosphere of beautiful ambience.
3) The little boy with big, beautiful eyes: He chose a McDonald's fast-food venue. I clearly remember his remarkable ability to demonstrate and communicate the love he had for his families. The incredible sadness is the fact that his missing person's case is still unsolved. We continue to work with his beautiful Spirit Soul, helping him to send love and healing to everyone who has been traumatised by his disappearance.

Grids

A crystal grid is used to help manifest a desired intention. Because it is physical, it visually displays your intention to the source.

A grid can also be created using flowers, candles, feathers, pictures and of course, crystals.

From my perspective, I am guided by my intuition when I choose the crystals for each ***assisted transition***.

The layout of the grid can be a pattern or a symbol. Being instinctively creative with this part of the process is a way to personalise the Soul's assisted transition. Whilst many people in the metaphysical industry will argue that there is a protocol for the assembling of a grid, for me, it's all about helping the Spirit Soul who is seeking assistance. Being of service to the Spirit World is not textbook; it's about the relationships and communication that Earth Souls and Spirit Souls create and nurture between the two realms.

Sacred space

Sacred space is any space or area that has been dedicated to a sacred purpose, in this case, "transitions." Therefore, the venue where we hold these ***assisted transitions*** becomes sacred space. This gives the Spirit a sense of protection and safety, where there is no negativity.

Celebrate their completed journey home to their Spiritual home

Honouring the Spirit Souls' completed transition is an essential part of the ceremony. The way we do this is through a thoughtful celebration. It is necessary to point out that some of the ***assisted***

transitions I've done have been highly emotional occasions, so when I say I honour and celebrate, I say this with enormous respect and love for these beautiful Souls.

Usually, the celebration will entail enjoying lovely food and drink with lots of fond chatter, as we compose our notes of the occasion, farewelling them at their departure.

On occasion, there have been some Spirit Souls who did not complete their proposed ***assisted transition***. As a Spiritual Medium who specialises in this field, I always continue to provide ongoing support to them. Always happy to be of service to the Spirit World, I always make myself available when they decide on another attempt to complete their journey back home to their Spirit Soul home.

While energies are high during transition, afterwards when all is done, you can sometimes feel drained and exhausted.

Dear departing Earth soul, as you step through the celestial departure doorway, remember, "We will see you later!" Meanwhile, we promise to stay in touch.

– Cheryl Kay

STEPPING THROUGH THE CELESTIAL DOORWAY

This platform originated out of love and a deep desire to look after Souls that get lost or stuck between worlds – the Earth's atmosphere and the Spirit World.

The ritual lighting of the candles symbolises blessing the chosen place for the event to take place.

The ritual of burning white sage incense to clear any residual negative energy from the space also creates a sanctuary for the Spirit Soul and Earth Soul to communicate.

Invocation for opening the sacred space

Love and protection to…

Winds of the South:

The element of fire, and Spiritual heart, we call upon you to wrap your golden healing light around us as we prepare for assisted transition through to the bright white light.

Winds of the West:

The element of water, and sacred womb, we call upon you to bathe us in a sea of compassion, peacefulness, and integrity as we prepare to assist the Spirit Soul's transition.

Winds of the North:

The element of Earth, our sacred body, we call upon you to assist us with our gift of intuition with this assisted transition: to know when to listen and when to speak. We listen with gratitude as you whisper your wisdom and guidance to us, to help this Spirit Soul complete their journey through to the love and light of their Spiritual home.

Winds of the East:

The element of air, and sacred breath, we call upon you to wrap your protective wings around us and the Soul who is seeking help for their journey home.

To Mother Earth:

As we receive your healing energy, we honour you; we thank you.

To Father Sun and Grandmother Moon:

As we align our mind and body Soul with your energy, we celebrate our healing; we thank you.

The sacred space is now ready. We are free to communicate, validate and connect with the Spirit Soul seeking help.

Invocation for closing the sacred space

Thank you for your love and protection…

Winds of the South:

Thank you for the healing light you brought us today.

Winds of the West:

Thank you for protecting our sacred space today. We embrace your wisdom on the journey the Soul takes beyond the Earth's atmosphere.

Winds of the North:

Thank you for your gracious guidance today. We applaud your skilful communication.

Winds of the East:

Thank you for assisting us today by creating a perfect flight plan/path for the Soul seeking our help.

To Mother Earth:

Thank you for the abundance of healing energy today.

To Father Sun and Grandmother Moon:

Thank you for your attention to detail during today's assisted transition. Awesome job.

Protective energy surrounds my Earth Soul.

I appreciate you sharing your energy with me today.

The extinguishing of the lit candles symbolises the completion of the ceremony.

My gift of a crystal to you signifies a thousand tender thoughts, eternal love, and a keepsake for your soul's journey home.

– Cheryl Kay

HEALING CRYSTALS FOR FRAGILE HEARTS

These crystals are helpful before, during and after transition.

Amethyst: Releases and assists with dissolving our physical Earth Soul bodies as we embark on our journey back to our Spiritual home – the transformation back to our Spirit Soul. This crystal is helpful for Earth Souls experiencing a gradual transition.

Aquamarine: Supports the Earth Soul to become ready to transition. They experience a calmer, less fearful feeling regarding their departure.

Carnelian: Protects the Earth Soul on its journey back to the Spirit World, to a newly evolved Life/Afterlife.

Chiastolite: We consider this crystal sacred. Supports the Soul's transition journey using high Spiritual energy.

Kunzite: Lilac kunzite opens the celestial doorway to Life/Afterlife. Assists with their transition – their journey through the seven heavenly halls, into the light.

Kyanite: Helps those Earth Souls who are experiencing a gradual transition. Beneficial in alleviating the Earth Soul's fears before their transition.

*Music gives our Earth soul wings to communicate
with the Spirit realm.*

– Cheryl Kay

MUSIC FOR BOTH SIDES OF THE VEIL

On numerous occasions, when I first wake up, there is a Spirit present who gently reminds me that it's a new day, a fresh start.

"Great, fantastic, brilliant," is my animated reply. Being a grateful recipient of their message, I always endeavour to respond with a message back to them in appreciation.

One of my favourite ways to do this is through music. Uplifting music holds tremendous vibration energy. Connecting to the Spirit World through music is a fantastic way to keep the communication lines open.

Listed below are a few of my favourite songs to play for them. I also sing along. It's one of the loveliest gifts you can share with your family and friends who have transitioned back to their Spiritual home.

Music also has healing capabilities. It can assist those who are grieving a recent transition of a loved one. A lovely way to connect and get your message across is through music. I recommend playing their preferred genre of music to connect to their energy. Alternatively, any music piece that connects the two

of you emotionally will be okay. To be 100 per cent effective, I highly recommend that you sing along.

I see your faces cringing, frowns etched firmly on your foreheads. Hey, guys, get over yourselves; sing that song and send that love to your family, friends, Spirit guides, Angels and your Spirited team of advisors. They will be so joyful, so happy.

Light a candle and reflect on the good times you shared. Make a playlist of their favourite music and music that reminds you of them. Always remember:

We don't say goodbye and neither do they. Instead, we say, "See you later!"

xoxo

Here is a list of some of the songs that I sing. xoxo
"Angels" – Robbie Williams
"Hello Again" – Neil Diamond
"You Raise Me Up" – Josh Groban
"From a Distance" – Bette Midler
"A Hundred Thousand Angels" – Lucinda Drayton
"Supermarket Flowers" – Ed Sheeran
"Everybody Hurts" – R.E.M.
"Dancing in the Sky" – Dani and Lizzy
"There You'll Be" – Faith Hill
"Tears in Heaven" – Eric Clapton
"Follow the Sun" – Xavier Rudd
"Spirit in the Sky" – Norman Greenbaum

A lighthouse beams rays of bright light and guidance without prejudice.

– Cheryl Kay

THE LIGHTHOUSE KEEPER FOR UNSETTLED SOULS

Heart-warming words to me from talented Spirit Medium Judy:

Cheryl, you are like the lighthouse for the ships in the night! Your beacon of light shines out to all misplaced Souls as you share messages, give guidance, and assist Souls in crossing over.

Thank you, Judy; such a lovely analogy.

I do see myself as a lighthouse for the Spirit Realm. Spirits are drawn to my energy, seeking assistance for their Soul, or seeking help to provide healing for their loved ones left behind when they transitioned.

Every Earth soul arrives with an exclusive blueprint plan – it incorporates helpful people and resources to complete a physical life of living and learning.

– Cheryl Kay

EXPLORING HELPFUL RESOURCES

The following list of resources is useful to access information that may assist you with your Earth Soul journey.

Websites

Louise Hermann: http://louisehermann.com/
Jason McDonald: http://jasonSpirit.com/
Sara King: http://saraking.com.au/

www.ingramcontent.com/pod-product-compliance
Lightning Source LLC
Chambersburg PA
CBHW041308110526
44590CB00028B/4286